THE
INVISIBLE WORLD
OF THE
INFRARED

THE INVISIBLE WORLD OF THE INFRARED

Jack R. White

Illustrated with photographs and drawings

DODD, MEAD & COMPANY • NEW YORK

PICTURE CREDITS

AGA Corporation, Sweden, 87; EROS Data Center, Sioux Falls, SD, 74, 75; General Dynamics Corporation, Fort Worth, TX, 93; General Electric Research and Development Center, Schenectady, NY, 119; General Electric Space Sciences Division, Philadelphia, PA, 71; Heath Company, Benton Harbor, MI, 115; Honeywell Electro Optics Division, Boston, MA, 89; Jet Propulsion Laboratory, Pasadena, CA, 60, 65; National Oceanic and Atmospheric Administration, Washington, DC, 80; Northrup Corporation, Electro-Mechanical Division, Anaheim, CA, 85; Raytheon Laser Center, Burlington, MA (reproduced by Larry Wadsworth), 100, 103; Raytheon Missile Systems Division, Lowell, MA, 95, (reproduced by Larry Wadsworth), 96, 97; Larry Wadsworth, Santa Barbara, CA, 26, 29. Drawings by Valerie Temple, 32, 33, 38, 47, 49, 51, 58, 109. All other photographs and diagrams are by the author.

1   2   3   4   5   6   7   8   9   10

Library of Congress Cataloging in Publication Data

White, Jack R.
The invisible world of the infrared.

Includes index.
Summary: Discusses what infrared is; how it is used in
science, in space, in the military, and in lasers today;
and its incredible possibilities in the future.
1. Infrared radiation—Juvenile literature.
2. Infrared technology—Juvenile literature. [1. Infrared
radiation. 2. Infrared technology] I. Title.
QC457.W45 1984   535.8′42   83-25441
ISBN 0-396-08319-6

Acknowledgments

Special thanks go to Valerie Temple for her many original ideas on how to draw the invisible, and to Risa Selig of the Electro-Optics Division of Honeywell, Inc. for invaluable help in providing research material and photographs.

To ROSS OLNEY, who showed me how to turn dreams into books, and to my wife, JUNKO, and children, JOHN and JENNY, who gave their love and encouragement and weekends to help the dream come true.

Contents

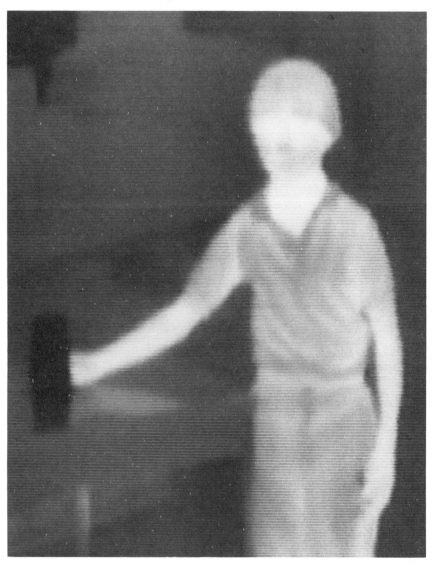

In the infrared, your body shines like a light bulb and a glass of ice water looks as black as tar.

ONE

The Invisible World

YOU ARE in a strange, glowing room where everything seems to be lit from inside with an eerie light. You try to look out the window, but the glass is a solid black. You press your hand against the cold window pane and leave a glowing print on the glass. Surprised, you look at your hands and find that they are shining, too.

The brightness from everything glowing hurts your eyes. You switch off the room lights, but nothing changes. You can see that the lights are turned off, but the room is as bright as ever.

You look behind you and see that you have left a trail of glowing footprints across the floor. You pick up the glass of ice water you left on the table. The water is as black as tar. Even the ice cubes are black.

"What is this place? Where am I?" you ask.

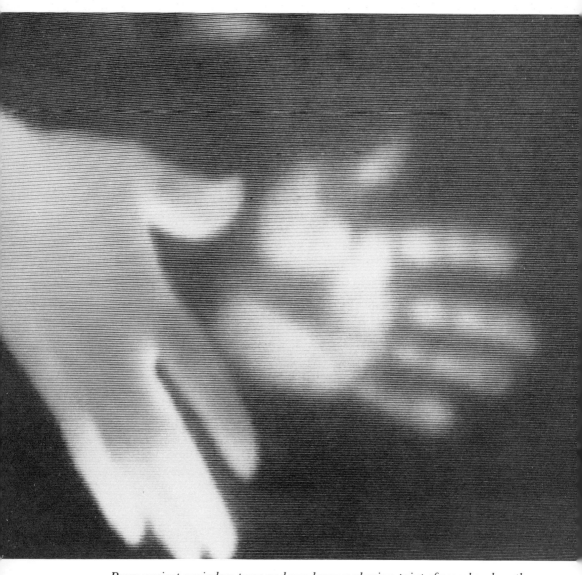

Press against a window pane and you leave a glowing print of your hand on the glass.

16

You are not in a science fiction story. You are seeing your own home the way it looks in the world of invisible light known as the infrared. This strange, shining world begins just below the red limit of our vision (the word "infra" means below). By themselves, our eyes can't see infrared rays. Special cameras are needed to change the invisible infrared into visible pictures.

Though you can't see infrared rays, you have felt them many times. When you warm your hands before a fire or a heater, it is infrared that you feel. Infrared rays are sometimes called "heat rays" because they are sent out by anything that is warm. The warmer the object, the stronger are its rays.

Because every person and every object sends out infrared rays from its own heat, no other light source (such as the sun or an electric light) is needed with infrared cameras. Things can be seen in total darkness. Any time there is a need to see in the dark, there is a need for the infrared. Engineers, scientists, soldiers, and spies all use infrared in their work.

LOOKING UP

From the tops of mountains in Arizona, California, and Hawaii, and from satellites in space, astronomers are using infrared to discover how stars are made. Large telescopes fitted with sensitive infrared instruments (instead of ordinary cameras or a person's eye) collect and analyze the infrared rays from interstellar clouds.

Interstellar (meaning "between the stars") clouds are clouds of gas and dust drifting in the empty regions of space. Astronomers believe that new stars are born from these clouds. Using infrared, they are able to see deep into interstellar clouds that blind ordinary telescopes.

Looking Down

Circling the earth once every 99 minutes, Landsat 4, the newest earth resources satellite, sends infrared pictures of earth taken from space down to receiving stations around the world. These pictures are being used to tell us how to take better care of our planet.

Differences between healthy and sick plants that can't be seen with the eye show clearly in the infrared. From studies of pictures taken of the same place over several years' time, scientists can tell if pollution or disease is hurting forests and crops.

In Saudi Arabia, infrared satellite pictures have been used to search for water under the desert sands by seeing the differences in plant life growing on the surface. In Canada, satellite pictures have been used to learn how acid rain from pollution has hurt the forests. In India, they have helped tell how much water will flow down to the plains from melting snow in the Himalaya Mountains.

Infrared satellites have advanced the new science of remote sensing (seeing and studying the world from a distance) to watch over the air, water, and food resources we need for life.

Today's War

In the sky over the Middle East, an American-made F-16 jet fighter belonging to Israel battles a Russian-made MiG-23. The two planes twist and turn in a dogfight, each trying to get into firing position before the other. The F-16 carries a "Sidewinder" infrared-guided missile mounted on each wing tip. The MiG-23 has two AA-8 "Aphid" infrared missiles under its belly.

The smaller, lighter F-16 is able to turn inside the MiG and brings the other plane into its sights. The F-16 pilot suddenly hears an angry, high-pitched whine in his headphones that tells him the infrared sensors in his missiles see the hot jet engine of the MiG. He pressses the launch button and the two missiles streak away. Twin trails of smoke snake across the sky following every turn and dive of the MiG. Then a ball of fire erupts as the missiles' warheads explode on target.

In the 1982 war over Lebanon, Israeli fighter planes

shot down over fifty Syrian MiG-21s and MiG-23s with Sidewinders. No Israeli planes were lost in air-to-air fighting.

TOMORROW'S WAR

From the edge of space, infrared sensors in a secret spy satellite detect the launch of hundreds of missiles from an enemy country. The war everyone fears has begun. The alarm is flashed down to earth where defenses are made ready.

As the first missiles rise out of the atmosphere carrying their deadly atomic warheads, something strange begins to happen. One by one, their nose cones are burned away. Blinded and out of control, they begin to tumble wildly. Most do not explode at all. A few blow up harmlessly thousands of miles from their targets. What has happened?

In this scene from the future, the missiles were shot down with the newest of space age weapons, the high-energy laser. All of the big countries of the world are working on these lasers that one day may be the main defense against missiles.

Unlike the red or green lasers seen in science fiction movies, real high-energy lasers are infrared. Infrared lasers are doubly dangerous because their beams are invisible.

LOOKING AHEAD

In war and in peace, in space and on earth, the infrared affects us all. In the future, it will become more and more a part of our everyday lives.

Robots that can see in the dark with infrared eyes will drive our cars, guard our homes, and do our housework. In the future, seeing in the infrared may be as easy as slipping on a pair of special glasses.

Our use of infrared is changing the world that we live in and perhaps changing us also. Our sense of sight is the main window that connects our minds with the world. With the help of infrared cameras and instruments, we are opening this window wider every day.

TWO

Things Weird and Wonderful

WHEN IS a window like a wall? Or ice cubes black? Or hot water glowing? How can you make your teeth turn black in an instant?

These aren't riddles. These are the way familiar, everyday things look in the infrared. For the most part, hot things shine and cold things look black.

Imagine you have a pair of infrared goggles that lets you see into the far-infrared. Put them on now and look into this world. What are some of the things that you see?

The first thing you may notice is that the windows have disappeared. They have all been replaced by shiny, black panels. In the far-infrared, glass isn't clear anymore. If it is cool—and most glass is cool because visible light rays pass through instead of being soaked up by the glass—then a window looks black. If it is heated, then the glass glows just like your body.

Look at yourself in the mirror. Wait a minute. Where did the mirror go? Being made of glass, ordinary mirrors look black, too. Mirrors made for the infrared have to be shiny on the outside. But you do get enough reflection from the surface of the glass of an ordinary mirror to see yourself even with the glass being black.

If you happen to be wearing glasses, of course they are black too, so take them off. You probably don't recognize the strange creature looking back at you. For one thing, it doesn't have any eyes. In the infrared, your eyes and the skin of your face look about the same since they are about the same temperature. Your nose and cheeks are darker because they are usually cooler than the other parts of your face.

Breathe in through your nose. Did you see your nostrils turn black? Spooky, isn't it? Now, smile. That's good. Now breathe in through your mouth and watch your teeth suddenly turn black as the air cools them. Ugh.

"Is that really me?" you may ask.

It is not only glass that isn't clear in the far-infrared. Water isn't either. Like glass, cool water looks black and warm water glows. Dip your hand in cold water and, for a

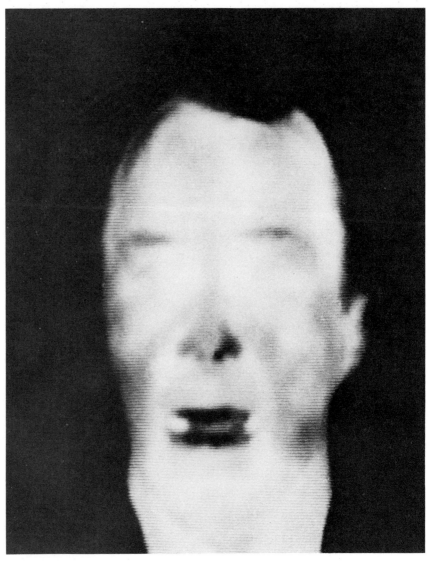

A human face in the infrared looks like a Halloween monster with black teeth and black nostrils and no eyes.

Cold water looks black. Dip a hand in and for a few seconds it looks as if you are wearing a black glove.

few seconds, it looks like you are wearing a black glove. Pour hot water over your hand and it looks like liquid gold.

If cold water is black, you can guess what ice cubes look like. That's right. Just like lumps of coal.

Not everything stops being clear in the infrared. There

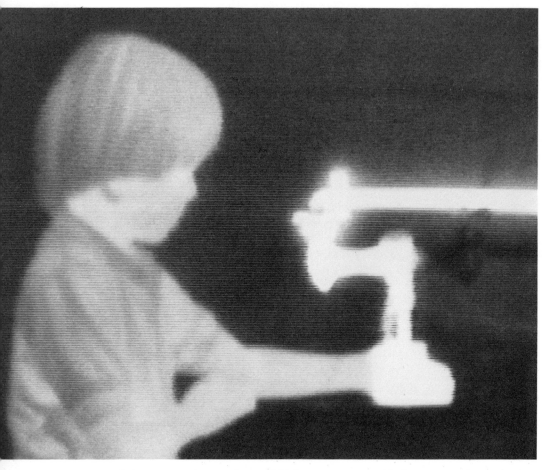

A hot water pipe on the wall lights up a corner of the room and warm water pours over your hand like liquid gold.

are some materials that you can't see through in the visible, but they make great windows and lenses in the infrared. Two of these are silicon and germanium, the same materials that transistors are made of. To your eye, they look as black as a slab of stone, but in the infrared they are almost invisible.

What are some of the other things that you see around you? Look at that coffee cup. In the infrared, you could use a hot cup of coffee to light up a corner of your room. At least until the coffee cooled.

Sometimes it looks like you can see through things. The water level in a metal or plastic bucket shows as plainly as if the bucket were clear. It's not, but the water cools the bucket, so everything below the water line is black while everything above glows the same as other room-temperature objects.

Looking at yourself and at things in the infrared is fun. It is also a reminder that you live in many worlds at the same time. In the same instant, you can be good-looking in any visible light and be a Halloween monster with black teeth and no eyes in the infrared.

This weird world that is as close to you as your own body is totally invisible. It surrounds you. It touches you. It is like the wind: you can feel its power, but you cannot see it. Only with special cameras and instruments can we make our senses reach into this world.

While no human can see infrared, there is one kind of animal on earth that can. Do you know which one it is?

27

Glass is clear to our eye, but germanium is a solid, shiny black. In this visible photo, the little girl can be seen through the glass she is holding, but the boy's face is hidden behind a piece of germanium.

28

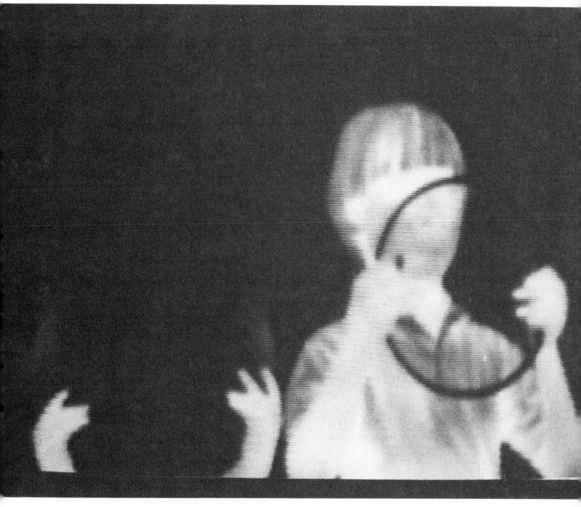

In the infrared, the opposite happens: The glass hides the girl's face, but the boy can be seen through the germanium.

29

THREE

Eyes of Planet Earth

ALL HUMANS are partly blind. Rays of energy pour out from the sun and the stars and from lightning and light bulbs, and our eyes see only a tiny part that we call visible light.

What we see, or rather, what we are unable to see, controls much of the way we live and the way we use the resources of our planet. Our eyes are made for sunlight. During the day we are (or believe we are) masters of the earth. But when the sun goes down, we become troubled by one of our oldest and deepest fears: our fear of the dark. Without light, we can't see and we are afraid of the dangers that may be hiding in the darkness.

To fight this fear, we flood our homes and buildings with electric light from light bulbs. We light up the night much brighter than is needed just to get around or to do our work. Turning on the lights at night is so familiar and seems so natural that we usually don't stop to wonder why we are doing it. Making the energy for all this light burns up a huge amount of oil and coal every year. If we could see in the infrared, we wouldn't need this artificial light.

Snake Sensors

When you see, your eyes make an image or picture of the scene in front of you in much the same way that a film camera does. No eyes on earth, either ours or those of animals, are able to see true images in the infrared, but some types of snakes have very sensitive infrared sensors that can tell the direction to a warm object. The best-developed sensors belong to snakes known as "pit vipers." Rattlesnakes are one kind of pit viper.

Pit vipers have a small hole (the pit) on each side of their head just below the normal eye. A thin piece of skin stretches across the back of each pit, something like the eardrum in one of your ears. This skin is covered with nerve endings that are very sensitive to any changes in temperature. If the warm body of a person or an animal moves in front of the snake, the infrared rays warm this skin, the same as your hands are warmed by a fire, but with thousands of times more sensitivity.

Having each skin sensor at the back of a pit, so that it is

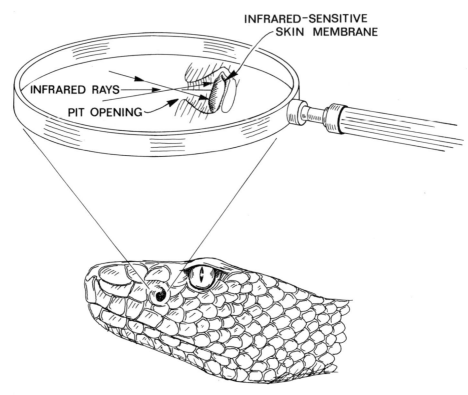

INFRARED-SENSITIVE
SKIN MEMBRANE

INFRARED RAYS

PIT OPENING

Rattlesnakes have sensitive infrared sensors in a small hole below each eye.

looking out through a kind of tunnel, allows the snake to see objects that are ahead and a little to the side. There is a small place right in front of the snake's head that can be seen by both of the sensors.

The two sensors work together to give the snake a sense of direction. By turning its head back and forth to balance the rays received by each pit, a rattlesnake can find even

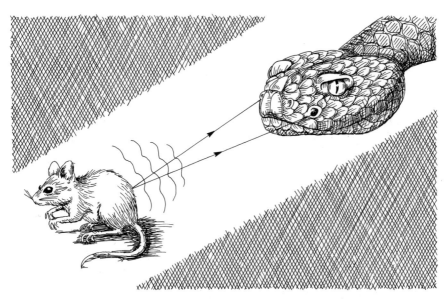

The sensors "see" in a cone-shaped view ahead of the snake. By balancing the rays received by each pit sensor, the snake can find mice and other prey in the dark.

small prey like mice in complete darkness and strike at them accurately.

In daylight, the snake's normal eyes send pictures to its brain just as our eyes do. Even when there is light enough to see with its eyes, the snake still uses the pit sensors to help it find food and to protect itself from enemies. The snake's visual sight and infrared sense help each other in much the same way as our sense of hearing helps our sight to warn us if a car is coming when we are walking and tells us the general direction of the danger.

33

Because the sensors in the pits are sensitive only to changes in the infrared rays striking them, any movement by the prey only makes it easier for the snake to find it. The old advice to "freeze" if you discover a rattlesnake close by makes good sense, especially if you could make your body cold as well as still.

Electronic Eyes

The cameras and instruments and weapons we build for the infrared often copy the way eyes and sensors work in nature. Sometimes an image like that made by our eyes is needed, as when we want to see patterns or shapes. For other uses, an image may not be necessary.

Sometimes we may want to use the rays that an object sends out to measure its temperature or to tell what it is made of. With infrared, this can be done from far away. This can be very handy if the object happens to be a star.

In the next chapter, we will find where our eyes are located on a map of light and see why some objects send out light that can be seen and others send only invisible infrared.

FOUR

The Invisible Rainbow

RAINBOWS ARE among nature's most beautiful sights. A rainbow is formed when tiny droplets of water in the air break beams of white sunlight apart into all of the colors our eyes can see, and more. And more? Yes, much more. Around the outside of every rainbow you see there is an invisible rainbow of infrared.

If we could see this invisible rainbow, would it be as beautiful as the one we know? We will never know for certain. No instrument can make our eyes see colors they were not designed for. The best that can be done is to change the wavelengths of light that are outside our senses into the colors that we can see.

Color is the way our eyes and minds respond to different wavelengths of light. Light can be thought of as a wave of energy traveling through space the way a wave of

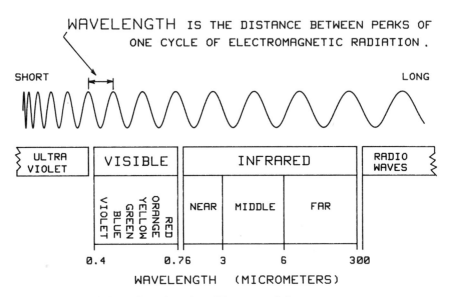

WAVELENGTH IS THE DISTANCE BETWEEN PEAKS OF ONE CYCLE OF ELECTROMAGNETIC RADIATION .

Wavelengths of the infrared and visible parts of the spectrum.

water travels through the ocean. The wavelength is the distance from the top of one wave to the next: the length of one wave.

Wavelengths of light are incredibly tiny. In the infrared, wavelengths are measured in units of micrometers (often called "microns" for short). It takes one million micrometers to make one meter. (Micro means one millionth of something.) The wavelengths of visible light are even smaller. They are measured either in nanometers or in angstroms. One nanometer is 1,000 times smaller than a micrometer and one angstrom is 10,000 times smaller.

Wavelengths are important because there is a connection between wavelength and energy. The shorter the wavelength of the light, the greater the energy it has. Radio waves, microwaves, infrared rays, visible light, ultraviolet light, X-rays, and gamma rays are all forms of electromagnetic radiation. Only their wavelengths and energies are different.

Wavelength can be thought of as a kind of address where a ray's energy is located. A map of all of the wavelengths of electromagnetic radiation is called a spectrum.

WHY CAN'T WE SEE IN THE DARK?

All warm objects (including our own bodies) send out energy in the form of electromagnetic radiation. If everything is sending out all this energy, why can't we see things like people and houses in the dark? In fact, why is it dark at all? The answer to both questions is that we are not able to see in the wavelengths where the energy from these objects lie.

When you see a person, you are seeing *reflected* light that has come from another source, such as the sun or a light bulb, and has bounced off the person's clothes and skin before it reached your eye. Except for a few kinds of sources such as lasers or phosphors (phosphors are used to make televsion screens), an object must be very hot before we can see direct light from it.

There is a direct connection between the temperature

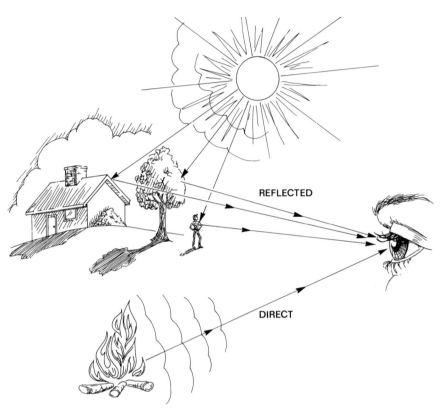

Cool things are seen by reflected light from the sun or from another light source. Very hot things are seen by the direct light they make.

of an object and the wavelengths of the energy it sends out. Cool to warm objects radiate all of their energy at long wavelengths, outside the visible wavelengths we are able to see. As the temperature of an object gets hotter, two things happen to the energy it is sending out: the energy gets stronger and it also shifts toward shorter wavelengths.

38

When an object reaches about 700 degrees Celsius (1,292 degrees Fahrenheit), the first wavelengths of its energy begin to enter the visible and we can start to see the object glowing a dull, reddish-orange color. This is about the temperature of hot coals or the grill on an electric range or heater.

If the temperature keeps getting hotter, the color changes to orange, then to yellow, and finally to white as the rays of energy completely cover the visible wavelengths. White light, such as sunlight, contains all of the visible wavelengths (all of the colors we can see).

Even though the peak of an object's energy shifts toward shorter wavelengths as it gets warmer, it still sends out energy at all the longer wavelengths, including infrared, microwaves, and radio waves.

The warmth of your body makes you more than a source of infrared rays. You are sending out radio waves as well. If the cold of outer space were around you, a sensitive receiver like those used for radio astronomy could hear you. Unfortunately, you wouldn't be very interesting to listen to since you are only sending out noise.

WINDOWS IN THE SKY

Before we can see something, the light from a source has to have a clear path to travel through to reach our eyes.

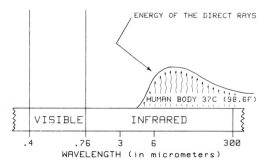

Our eyes can't see people and room-temperature objects in the dark because almost all of their direct rays are in the far-infrared.

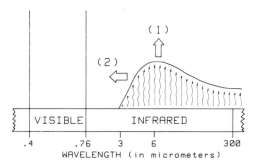

When the temperature of an object gets hotter, two things happen: (1) The energy of its rays becomes stronger (so it looks brighter). (2) The energy moves toward the visible wavelengths.

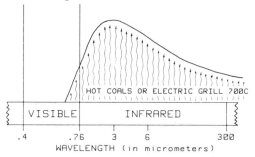

At about 700 degrees Celsius, the rays from an object reach the visible and we see a reddish-orange glow.

40

Usually the light rays must pass through the mixture of gases in the atmosphere that we call "air." The main gases in air are nitrogen, oxygen, argon, carbon dioxide, and water vapor (water that has changed from a liquid to a gas).

Except on foggy or hazy days, we usually don't think about air not being clear, because the visible part of the spectrum is in the middle of what scientists call an atmospheric "window." Atmospheric "windows" are completely different from the glass windows we are used to. Atmospheric windows are wavelength regions in the spectrum where the air lets rays of light or infrared pass without absorbing them or scattering them in different directions.

There are many atmospheric windows scattered throughout the spectrum, but most of the atmospheric windows in the infrared are not as clear as the one we have in the visible. In between these windows, there are deep "absorption regions." These are wavelength regions where most or all of the rays from a source are absorbed, "soaked up," by the molecules of the gases in the air. Carbon dioxide and water vapor cause most of the absorption in the infrared. In space, where there is no air, there are no absorption regions.

If you could look into one of these absorption regions, it would be like being inside a thick, black, fog. Even using a bright light, the farthest you could see would be only 20 or 30 feet.

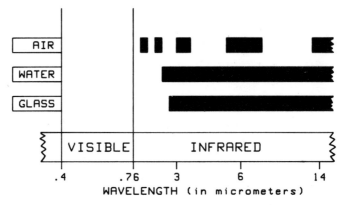

Some materials are clear in the visible, but block infrared. Air has clear "windows" scattered across the spectrum. Water and glass absorb all of the middle and far-infrared wavelengths.

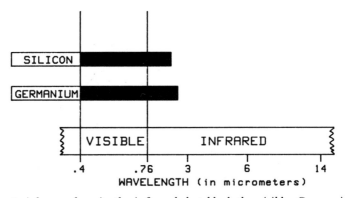

Some materials are clear in the infrared, but block the visible. Germanium and silicon both make excellent lenses for infrared cameras.

THINGS THAT SEE INFRARED

There are many different kinds of instruments and cameras that can "see" at infrared wavelengths. The choice of which to use usually depends upon the source to be seen.

Like our eyes, most instruments see only a narrow wavelength region. To be useful, an instrument must be sensitive in the wavelength region where the rays from the source are located and this region must have an atmospheric window.

Four of the main instruments that are sensitive to infrared are:

1. Infrared film
2. Guided missiles
3. Imaging systems
4. Scientific instruments for research

Infrared film is sensitive in the visible and the near-infrared. The long wavelength limit of film is about .9 micrometers. This isn't far enough into the infrared to see direct rays from people and room-temperature sources. Like our eyes, film needs reflected light from the sun or some other source.

Infrared film is very useful for studying plants. The leaves of healthy plants are reflective in the near-infrared. This makes them look very bright in infrared photographs. Diseased plants loose their reflections in the infrared and look dull and dark.

Infrared missiles that are designed to shoot down airplanes are sensitive to wavelengths between about 2 to about 5 micrometers where the infrared rays from jet aircraft are strongest.

Missiles that are designed for ground targets, like tanks, trucks, and ships, usually see in the 8 to 14 micrometer atmospheric window. These targets are a lower temperature than aircraft, so their rays are at longer wavelengths.

Infrared imaging systems change an infrared scene into a picture that our eyes can see. This picture is usually shown on an ordinary television set. Most infrared imaging systems are made to be sensitive in the 8 to 14 micrometer window, so that they can see people and room-temperature objects.

There are many different kinds of scientific instruments that are made for wavelengths from the very short to the very long. Scientific instruments are different from other devices used in the infrared because they are usually designed to measure, rather than just to see. They find out how much energy is present and at what wavelengths it is located.

The instrument that was used to discover infrared was a simple, household item that had been around for two hundred years before anyone thought to use it to look for invisible light. You probably have one of these in your home right now. Can you guess what it is?

FIVE

Things That See in the Dark

How do you "see" infrared? First, you need something that is sensitive to infrared rays. You know that your skin can feel the rays, but only from objects that are very hot. Rattlesnakes are sensitive to infrared, but it wouldn't be very practical to build a camera or instrument out of a rattlesnake. Imagine having a camera that you had to feed.

What you need is something that changes in some measurable way when infrared strikes it. The change can be electrical, giving a signal like a television signal that can be made into a picture. It can be chemical, like the change that takes place in photographic film when it is exposed to light. Or the change can be physical, like the way mercury in a thermometer expands and moves up the glass tube when the temperature gets warmer.

THE FIRST INFRARED INSTRUMENT

Infrared rays were first discovered by using a thermometer. (Did you guess correctly?) In England in 1800, a scientist and astronomer named William Herschel experimented with sunlight, using a glass prism and a mercury thermometer much like the thermometers we still use.

Thermometers had been invented about two hundred years before by Galileo in Italy. And, about 135 years before, Sir Isaac Newton, the great English scientist, had used a prism to study the colors of light. Most people knew that the triangle-shaped block of glass known as a prism could break apart white sunlight into the spectrum of colors, just as a rainbow does. But until Herschel, no one had thought to put a thermometer and a prism together to try to measure the amount of heat in each color.

Herschel put his prism in a window to catch the sun's rays and shot the beam of colors onto a table across the darkened room. He placed the thermometer so that the bulb of mercury was in the colored light. Starting with violet, he moved the thermometer up, stopping at blue, green, yellow, orange, and finally at red. At each color, he carefully read the thermometer temperature and subtracted the temperature of the room (taken from a second thermometer), so that only the heat from the light was left.

Then a strange thing happened. He moved the ther-

The first infrared instrument was a glass prism and a mercury thermometer, used by William Herschel in 1800 to discover infrared rays in a beam of sunlight.

mometer beyond red and found that it still gave a reading where no light could be seen at all. Imagine how surprised and excited he must have been. He had not only discovered, he had actually measured, something completely invisible. It was almost as if he had photographed a ghost.

47

In later experiments, Herschel found that a temperature rise could be measured for other sources than the sun, in fact, from sources that were not glowing at all. He learned what we now know to be true: that it is possible for an object to give off infrared and not give off visible rays. So an instrument that can see infrared can see in total darkness.

OPTICS AND DETECTORS

The instrument Herschel made was very simple, but the idea and the basic design were exactly the same as many instruments used today. By putting together a prism and a thermometer, Herschel used the two parts that almost every infrared camera and instrument has today: optics and a detector.

Optics can be lenses, like those used in telescopes and magnifying glasses, or they can be mirrors or prisms or any number of other things. Anything that bends or reflects or separates different wavelengths of light can be called optics. For infrared wavelengths longer than about 2 micrometers, lenses are usually made of silicon or germanium rather than glass, or else they are made by using curved mirrors like the large telescopes used for astronomy.

Herschel's glass prism only let him measure the near-infrared, just below the visible. If he had known to use a different prism material, he would have found infrared

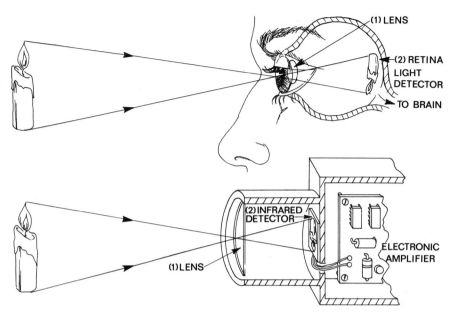

(1) LENS

(2) RETINA
LIGHT
DETECTOR

TO BRAIN

(2) INFRARED
DETECTOR

(1) LENS

ELECTRONIC
AMPLIFIER

The two main parts of our eye and of almost every infrared camera and instrument are: (1) optics (lenses or mirrors) to collect and image the rays, and (2) one or more detectors to sense them.

went much further than he imagined. Germanium and silicon weren't known in Herschel's time, but one material he could have used was salt. A prism made from a block of salt passes infrared very well, as long as you don't let it get wet!

A thermometer such as Herschel used has three problems as an infrared detector. It is not very sensitive. It is not automatic: A person is needed to read the numbers off the scale and write them down. A thermometer is too slow to follow a sudden change in the amount of infrared striking it.

Most detectors used today send an electrical signal out when infrared strikes them. They are thousands of times more sensitive than Herschel's thermometer and also can change their reading thousands of times faster. That is very important if you want to make a television picture of the far-infrared.

IMAGINE AN IMAGING MACHINE

When you look at anything, from a person to a pancake, your eye breaks the scene in front of you up into millions of tiny parts. The lens at the front of your eye makes an image on the sensitive retina at the back. The retina is made of millions of tiny detectors that are sensitive to light. Each detector sends a message through the optic nerve to tell your brain the brightness and color of the light striking the detector.

It is up to your brain to make sense out of all these milions of messages arriving at the same time. The image you see is something like a million-piece jigsaw puzzle, where each piece, each picture element, is so tiny that all it has on it is a dot of color. You can't tell anything from just one piece, but the supercomputer that is your brain puts the puzzle together in an instant.

An imaging system that sees in the infrared works in much the same way as your eye. It breaks a scene up into

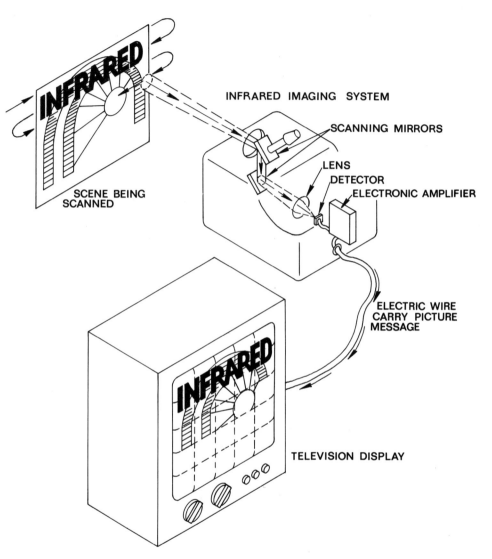

INFRARED IMAGING SYSTEM

SCANNING MIRRORS

LENS

DETECTOR

ELECTRONIC AMPLIFIER

SCENE BEING
SCANNED

ELECTRIC WIRE
CARRY PICTURE
MESSAGE

TELEVISION DISPLAY

An infrared imaging system scans a complicated scene, breaking it up into thousands of tiny pieces to be sent as electrical signals to a screen for viewing.

51

tiny parts, sends the messages to where the picture will be used, and puts the puzzle back together again. It isn't possible yet to make millions of tiny detectors like your eye has. Most infrared imaging systems have only a few or, sometimes, only one detector. They break a scene into tiny parts in a different way than your eye: They scan it.

With scanning, the detector sees only one part of the scene at a time. Spinning mirrors sweep the detector's view back and forth and up and down across the scene. As it scans, the detector sends out a message about the strength of the infrared rays it sees in each part of the scene.

Scanning breaks a complicated scene into a series of single picture elements that come out one after the other in time. This isn't nearly as good as having all of the picture elements at the same time (in parallel) as your eye does. Scanning takes a lot longer to put together a picture and also this kind of imaging system must have a lot of delicate and complicated mechanical parts. Imagine having a couple of spinning mirrors inside each of your eyes. The noise alone would be enought to give you a headache.

Getting the Message

As the train of electronic messages about the amount of infrared in each picture element is received, the puzzle is put together to make a picture our eyes can see. This is often done with an ordinary television set.

The electron beam in the television scans across the screen at the same time and same position (left to right and top to bottom) as the scanning done by the mirrors in the imaging system. This electron beam "paints" the messages from the infrared imaging system onto the screen as either spots of color or as light or dark spots (for a black-and-white picture). In this way, the invisible infrared is changed into a visible picture.

In the next chapters, we will follow some of the different kinds of infrared instruments into space and then back to earth again and see how infrared is being used to make our lives safer in some ways and more dangerous in others.

SIX

Infrared in Space: Looking Up

ASTRONOMY IS the oldest of the sciences. We know that people gazed at and knew the positions of the stars and planets long before the first recorded history. But infrared astronomy is one of the youngest and one of the most exciting branches of science today. It is an important tool in the search for answers to the "how" and the "why" of the universe.

An enormous amount of information about the stars and planets has been learned from the tiny slice of the spectrum that we can see. The infrared part of the spectrum is over eight hundred times wider than the visible. Even more information may be hidden there, waiting for astronomers with new, more sensitive instruments to discover.

Instead of a human eye or a film camera at the focus of the telescope, infrared astronomers use several different kinds of specialized instruments. Very little image work is done in infrared astronomy. Infrared imaging systems are not as advanced as those in the visible. Infrared imaging systems are not able to see small objects as sharply as visible photography can, so infrared pictures usually look "fuzzy."

Most infrared instruments are designed for measurement. They get numbers telling how strong the infrared rays received are, rather than make pictures. The two basic kinds of instruments are radiometers and spectrometers. A radiometer measures the amount of infrared received by the telescope within a band of wavelengths. A spectrometer separates the wavelengths of infrared, as a glass prism does in the visible, and makes a map of the amount of infrared received at each of the different wavelengths.

From the patterns of dark absorption "lines" in a spectrum, scientists can identify the elements in the star or dust cloud that was the source of the rays. The shape of the received spectrum tells them the temperature of the source. The position of the lines tells the speed the source is moving. From these kinds of information, scientists gather important clues to the conditions needed to form a new star or to destroy an old one.

There are many problems in seeing and measuring

infrared rays from planets and stars. Because infrared rays from the stars are very weak, very sensitive instruments are needed to see them. Much of the progress in infrared astronomy had to wait until the space age sciences of solid-state physics (how to make transistors and transistor materials) and cryogenics (how to make things very, very cold) were ready.

THE FIRST PROBLEM: SENSITIVITY

The materials used in modern infrared detectors sound like the names of planets or strange, foreign cities: Indium-antimonide and mercury-cadmium-telluride are among the two most often used. When cooled a few hundred degrees below freezing, these detectors become millions of times more sensitive than the thermometer Herschel used to discover infrared. To get the sensitivity needed to see the stars, a detector must be made as cold as possible. To a cold detector, everything around it looks hot.

Very cold temperatures are made by compressing a gas until it turns into liquid and then letting the liquid boil back into a gas. When a liquid changes into a gas, it soaks up heat from everything around it. The refrigerator in your home cools by doing this with a gas called Freon.

To cool infrared detectors, either liquid nitrogen or liquid helium are most often used. We talk about water being "boiling hot." These liquids are "boiling cold." Liquid nitrogen boils at 77 degrees Kelvin (minus 321 degrees on the Fahrenheit scale) and liquid helium boils at 4 degrees Kelvin (minus 452 degrees F). If you dipped a finger into boiling liquid nitrogen, it would freeze into a solid "fingercicle" in an instant.

Infrared detectors are usually built into the side or bottom of a vacuum thermos bottle. When the thermos bottle is filled with the liquified gas, the detector is kept at the temperature of the boiling liquid.

THE SECOND PROBLEM: EVERYTHING IS A SOURCE

One of the most useful features of infrared is being able to see room-temperature objects by their own rays. In astronomy, infrared becomes its own worst enemy. Once the detector is made highly sensitive, the next problem is the infrared rays coming from every part of the telescope itself.

The infrared rays from the mirrors and telescope body hide the weak rays from the stars. The longer the wavelength, the worse the problem. To get an understanding of this problem, imagine looking through a telescope where the mirrors were glowing red hot.

To separate the rays coming from the telescope from those of the star, infrared telescopes use a "wobbling" secondary mirror to make the telescope's view switch back and

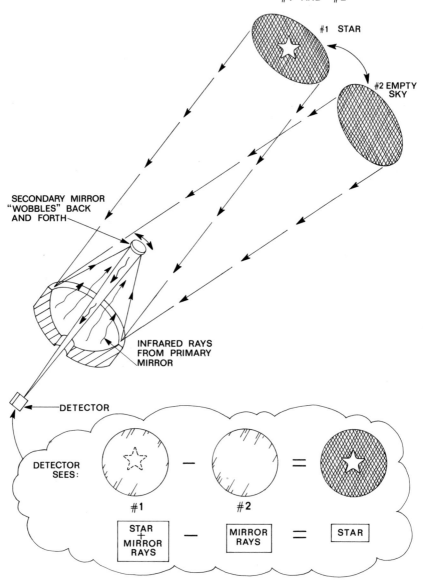

TWO VIEWING POSITIONS
#1 AND #2

#1 STAR

#2 EMPTY SKY

SECONDARY MIRROR "WOBBLES" BACK AND FORTH

INFRARED RAYS FROM PRIMARY MIRROR

DETECTOR

DETECTOR SEES:

#1   —   #2   =

STAR + MIRROR RAYS   —   MIRROR RAYS   =   STAR

forth between two parts of the sky. The telescope is pointed so that the star is in one viewing position and empty sky is in the other. The infrared detector at the focus of the telescope sees first the star, then empty sky, then the star again; back and forth, again and again.

The amount of infrared seen by the detector in the "empty sky" viewing position is subtracted from the amount of infrared seen in the "star" position. Since the unwanted rays from the telescope itself are the same in both viewing positions, most of them are accounted for by the subtraction. This helps, but doesn't completely solve the problem and it creates a new difficulty. Because it is switching back and forth, the detector "sees" the star less than half the time, so less than half the possible energy is received. This loss of sensitivity makes the telescope and detector unable to see dim stars that they could see if they were able to keep the star constantly in view.

The best way to get rid of the unwanted infrared is to cool the whole telescope to the same cold temperature as the detector. The problems with getting the mirror surfaces the same temperature all over and with keeping frost off the cold mirrors usually make this too difficult to do with earth-bound telescopes.

The mirrors of infrared telescopes on earth are made to "wobble" between the star and a nearby area of empty sky, so that rays from the telescope itself can be subtracted out.

Technicians ready the Infrared Astronomical Satellite, IRAS, for launch at Vandenberg Air Force Base, California.

THE THIRD PROBLEM: THE AIR WE BREATHE

The biggest problem of all is the atmosphere. The air that surrounds the earth, and makes life here possible, makes life miserable for infrared astronomers. There are only a few good atmospheric "windows" in the infrared. Water vapor, carbon dioxide, and ozone in the air absorb much of the other wavelengths, including those wavelengths where some of the most important information about stars is found.

To get above as much of the atmosphere as possible, astronomical telescopes are built on the tops of mountains. This helps, especially with water vapor, because the air at high altitude is very dry. Balloons, aircraft, and rockets have also been used, but the only way to solve the problem completely is to get above the atmosphere altogether. Looking at the far reaches of space in the infrared is best done from cold, airless space itself.

THE SATELLITE SOLUTION

On January 25, 1983, as storm clouds drifted in off the Pacific Ocean, the flame of a rocket booster lit up the lonely plain of Vandenberg Air Force Base on the California coast. Riding on a column of fire, the first satellite designed for infrared astronomy was launched into orbit around the earth.

The Infrared Astronomical Satellite (IRAS for short) is

the answer to the dreams of infrared astronomers around the world. Its main mission is to make an infrared map of the stars at longer wavelengths than possible from earth telescopes.

IRAS is the combined work of three countries: The United States built the telescope mirror and detectors, the Netherlands built the satellite body and electronics, and Britain is providing the receiving station for the pictures IRAS sends back to earth.

Being in space, IRAS is free of the problems that make infrared astronomy from the ground so difficult. The group of detectors, the mirror, and the telescope tube are all cooled with liquid helium. With only the emptiness of space all around, there are no gases to absorb the infrared rays from the stars or to scatter unwanted light from cities into its view.

The lifetime of IRAS depends on how long the supply of liquid helium lasts. After the coolant is gone, the detectors and telescope will become warm and IRAS will no longer be usable. By that time, it is hoped that IRAS will have completely mapped the skies in the infrared and provided information for astronomers to study for many years.

IRAS DISCOVERS A SOLAR SYSTEM

The main mission of IRAS is to make a map of the infrared sources in the sky. As a new instrument with a capability greater than any before, IRAS is certain to make many new, exciting discoveries beyond those of its basic mission. Already IRAS has found evidence of another solar system besides our own.

A solar system is a star and a group of planets and asteroids (asteroids are pieces of rock of all sizes) that circle in orbit around the star. Astronomers believe that many, perhaps most, of the stars we see have solar systems. The back and forth motion of one nearby star, called Barnard's star, is believed to be caused by the gravity field of a giant planet in its solar system, but no telescopes have been able actually to see planets or asteroids belonging to other stars before.

Planets are too cold to send out direct rays in the visible wavelengths. Visible astronomy can only see planets by the light they reflect from their star. This reflected visible light is too weak to see from the distance of the nearest star. The only planets we have actually seen are the ones in our own solar system.

While planets do not send out visible light, they are warm enough to be sources of infrared. Much of the early infrared astronomy studied the planets of our solar system. When the telescope in IRAS was pointed at the star Vega in August of 1983, an unexpectedly large amount of infrared for a star of Vega's size and type was measured. Astronomers believe this infrared is coming from a large ring or belt of asteroids and dust around Vega.

After the discovery by IRAS, an infrared astronomical telescope in a jet transport plane flying at 41,000 feet above the earth was also used to look at Vega. The measurement readings made by IRAS and by the aircraft telescope were found to be the same. The evidence of an infrared source around Vega was confirmed.

Vega is a very young star compared to our sun. It is less than 1 billion years old. Our sun is a middle-aged star 4.6 billion years old. Vega is believed to be too young for the asteroids and dust clouds around it to have had time to form full-sized planets yet. Astronomers will use this new discovery by IRAS to attempt to learn how solar systems are made.

From Dust to Dust: New Stars from Old

One of the most valuable uses of infrared is its power to see into clouds of dust that block the view of visible telescopes. An exploding star sometimes makes an enormous cloud of dust, called a circumstellar ("around a star") cloud. When this happens, most of the visible light given off by the star is absorbed by the dust. The dust is warmed by this light and radiates this energy at the longer wavelengths of the infrared.

Many of these stars are invisible to normal telescopes, but they are strong sources of infrared. The fine grains of dust shot into space by exploding stars become the material

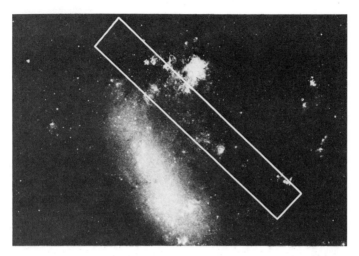

The Large Magellanic cloud is one of many clusters of stars and dust in the universe that may be the birthplace of new stars. The white box shows the region scanned by IRAS.

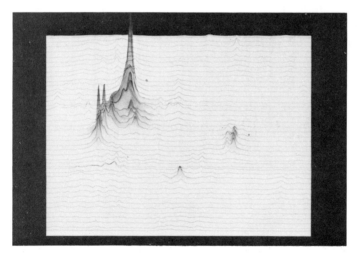

An infrared map of the Large Magellanic Cloud made by IRAS shows "peaks" of strong infrared from sources within the cloud. The stronger the infrared rays, the higher the peak drawn on the map.

to make new stars in a few billion years.

As clouds of interstellar ("between the stars") dust drift through space, the grains of dust sometimes begin to pull together. As more dust comes together, the pull of gravity becomes stronger on the surrounding dust and this "clumping together" becomes faster and faster, like a giant, black snowball rolling down an invisible "hill" of gravity. As the amount of dust grows, gravity squeezes it down and the pressure makes the dust get hotter and hotter.

As the temperature goes up, this baby star starts to radiate, first at radio wavelengths, then in the infrared, and finally in the visible. When the pressures and temperatures become great enough, thermonuclear reactions, like millions of atomic bombs, will feed the fires of the new sun.

Exactly how stars begin to grow and how they change from one kind of star to the next is not clearly understood. All stars do not seem to act the same way. Knowing more about the life and death patterns of stars is especially important, because it may let us know more about the future of our own star, the sun.

Where Do We Go from Here?
New telescopes and instruments like IRAS will give many clues to these mysteries, and the information brought back will also tell us how to build future instruments. That

information can sometimes be as important as the findings themselves.

New infrared satellites are being designed based on what has been learned from IRAS. In Germany, a satellite known as the German Infrared Laboratory is being built with a telescope and instruments ten times as sensitive as those in IRAS. It will be carried into space in the bay of the U. S. space shuttle in 1987. An American infrared telescope is being designed for launch in 1990, and a European infrared observatory in 1992.

In the next chapter, we will turn our telescopes around to look down at ourselves and our planet in the infrared.

SEVEN

Infrared in Space: Looking Down

As YOU READ this, your city is probably being watched by infrared "eyes" from space. Infrared satellites are the watchdogs of the twentieth century. They keep an ever-alert eye on our natural resources, our weather, and our defense.

Three main kinds of satellites carry infrared instruments to watch the earth from space: earth resources satellites, weather satellites, and military "spy" satellites.

LANDSAT: AN EARTH RESOURCES SATELLITE

On July 16, 1982, Landsat 4, the latest and largest earth resources satellite of its kind was launched into an orbit that passes over every part of the earth's surface (except for small areas around the north and south poles) once each eighteen days. From its viewpoint in space, Landsat 4 is busy scanning the earth to make visible and infrared pictures that are used by scientists, engineers, and cartographers (map makers) all over the world.

Landsat 4 travels in a nearly polar orbit around the earth, traveling from south to north to south again. The orbit is "sun-synchronous," meaning that it is carefully timed with the daily rotation of the earth and the yearly travel of the earth around the sun, so that the sun will be in the same position in the sky for each pass of the satellite. Keeping the local time of each satellite pass the same makes it possible to see long-term changes in the environment by comparing pictures taken over several seasons or even several years.

Landsat 1 was launched on July 23, 1972. It and Landsats 2 and 3 are in orbits 570 miles above the earth's surface. The instruments in Landsats 1 and 2 have finally failed after so many years in space and only part of Landsat 3 is still working. These first three satellites were designed to be used until they stopped working and then abandoned in space. Someday they will reenter the earth's atmosphere and burn up like meteors.

The Landsat 4 satellite was placed in a lower orbit, 438 miles high, so it could be brought down and captured by the space shuttle when the satellite needs to be repaired. The satellite will burn the hydrazine rocket fuel it has on board to propel it down to an orbit 100 miles lower where it can be reached by the space shuttle. Astronauts floating in space will repair the satellite and refuel the hydrazine tanks. Then it will be thrust back into the higher orbit.

THE LANDSAT IMAGING SYSTEMS

Landsat 4 carries two different imaging systems. Both systems use mirror telescopes with a group of visible and infrared detectors at the telescope focus. A flat mirror in each of the imaging systems rocks back and forth, causing the view of the telescope to scan back and forth like the sweep of a broom across the earth's surface.

The speed of this back-and-forth sweep is matched to the forward speed of the satellite, so a new patch of earth moves under the satellite on each sweep. In this way, a "strip" of earth 115 miles wide is constantly being scanned beneath the satellite.

The scenes scanned by the imaging systems are made into electrical signals and transmitted by radio down to receiving stations in countries all around the world. There, computers put the "jigsaw puzzle" of pieces together to make complete pictures.

The smaller imaging system in Landsat 4 is called the Multi-Spectral Scanner (or MSS for short). Landsats 1, 2, and 3 each carried an MSS. The MSS can see objects on the earth's surface that are about the size of a football field. It

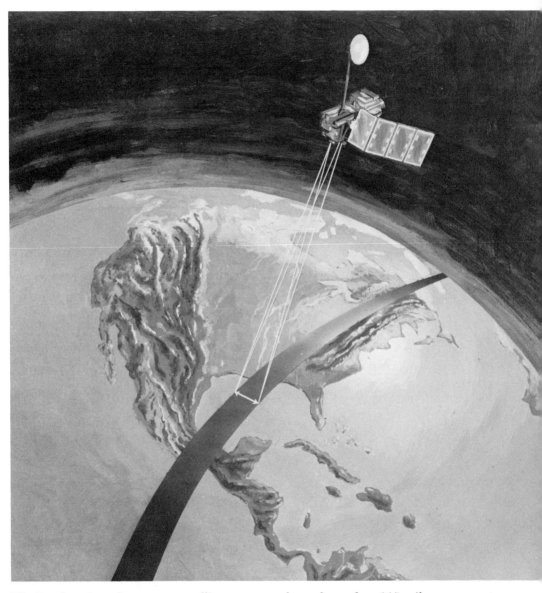

The Landsat 4 earth resources satellite scans a path on the surface 115 miles wide as it circles the earth.

71

has detectors that see in four different wavelength bands. Two of the bands are in the visible and two are in the infrared.

The larger imaging system on Landsat 4 is a completely new design. It is called the Thematic Mapper. It can see objects about three times smaller than the MSS. It has seven different wavelength bands. Three are in the visible and four are infrared.

MULTI-SPECTRAL POWER

Both the MSS and the Thematic Mapper aboard Landsat 4 are multi-spectral: They both "see" in several different wavelength bands in the visible and infrared parts of the spectrum. These different wavelength bands give Landsat its powerful ability to detect natural and man-made forces that affect the delicate balance of life on our planet.

The different wavelength bands were chosen for the different kinds of information to be found in each. The seven bands seen by the Thematic Mapper and some of their uses are:

1. The blue wavelength band (.45 to .52 micrometers) in the visible is best for mapping coastlines and for telling the difference between coniferous (evergreens such as pine trees) and deciduous trees (trees that loose their leaves in autumn).

2. The green wavelength band (.52 to .60 micrometers) in the visible is best for seeing water pollution, sediment particles in the water, and for mapping shallow water areas, such as shoals and reefs.

3. The red wavelength band (.63 to .69 micrometers) in the visible is best for telling the difference between city and country areas and between some different types of plants.

4. The near-infrared band (.76 to .90 micrometers) is best for viewing plant life. The leaves of healthy plants are highly reflective in these wavelengths, so they look very bright in a photograph.

5. The first mid-infrared band (1.55 to 1.75 micrometers) is used for measuring the amount of moisture in plant life and for telling the difference between clouds and snow.

6. The far-infrared band (10.4 to 12.5 micrometers) mainly sees direct infrared from the warm earth instead of reflected sunlight. The temperature patterns seen as the ground cools at night can be used to tell how much and how deep the moisture is in the soil and to tell different kinds of rock formations. This band can be used on the night side of earth.

7. The second mid-infrared band (2.08 to 2.35 micrometers) is used by geologists to identify different kinds of rock in the search for oil and other minerals.

New Orleans, Louisiana, seen from the Landsat 3 satellite in the green wavelength band of the visible.

THE SCIENCE OF REMOTE SENSING

Almost every branch of science and engineering has found remote sensing from space to be valuable. A few of

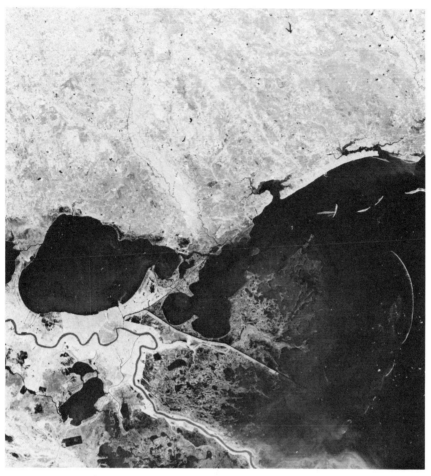

In the near-infrared, the land areas in the same scene look bright because of sunlight reflected off healthy plants, while the water looks darker than in the visible.

the uses in five branches of science are given below:

1. In agriculture and forestry, different kinds of crops and forest trees can be identified and plants that are under

stress from disease, pollution, or lack of water or nutrients can be detected. Maps showing the amount of land used for growing different kinds of crops can indicate how large a yearly harvest will be. Differences can be seen between dry soil and damp soil.

2. In geology, the view from space makes it possible to see patterns caused by some of the powerful forces that have been at work shaping the mountains and flatlands. Fault zones, cracks where earthquakes have shifted the earth's crust, can be found. Scars left by ancient glaciers can be seen over a whole region.

3. In water resources and oceanography, the amount of water in lakes and rivers and the amount of snow pack in the mountains can be measured to tell if there will be enough water for irrigation or if there will be floods. Layers of marine organisms that are the main food supply for ocean fish can be seen near the surface. Large icebergs in the ocean can be spotted, so that ships can be warned of danger.

4. In the environment, water and air pollution can be detected by the changes made in plant life or in the weather. The amount of forest land that has been cut down or burned or the area that has been strip-mined can be measured.

5. In cartography, maps are made from Landsat pictures that are more accurate, more up-to-date, and cost less

money than those made by ground surveying or photo-graphy from airplanes. Modern map making uses com-puters to draw maps from information stored in their memories. Landsat pictures are easy to use for making maps because their picture information is already in computer form.

Remote sensing is a fast-growing science. The Landsat pictures still contain much more information than we are able to understand and use right now. New discoveries and new uses for the satellite information are being made every day. The more we learn to understand what this and other earth resources satellites are telling us, the more valuable they will become.

WEATHER SATELLITES

Weather is one of the most powerful forces of nature. Airplanes and ships and sometimes our homes and lives are threatened by storms. Even when there are no big storms, too little or too much rain or too hot or too cold a tempera-ture can do enormous damage.

One of the first and perhaps the most important uses of man-made satellites was gathering pictures and other infor-mation for meteorologists to use to tell what the weather will be like. The satellite pictures you see on television weather

77

reports were radioed down to earth from a weather satellite in space over your area.

Unlike earth resources information, weather information is needed quickly and from many parts of the earth at once to spot storms developing and to tell the speed and direction they are moving. A satellite in space can take pictures of cloud patterns and make scientific measurements over large areas of the earth that would be impossible to cover with aircraft or ground weather stations.

Weather satellites of many different designs have been placed in orbit since the first TIROS (Television and Infra-Red Observation Satellite) was launched in April of 1960. These satellites are of two basic kinds: those that travel in polar, sun-synchronous orbits (like the orbit of Landsat) and those that are in geosynchronous (also called geostationary) orbits. Because of the different heights and directions of their orbits, the two kinds of satellites have very different views of the earth.

The sun-synchronous weather satellites circle the earth with their instruments and imaging systems scanning a wide path across the earth's surface. The latest of many TIROS and advanced TIROS satellites is the NOAA-8, launched on March 28, 1983. The imaging system in NOAA-8 has four wavelength bands: one in the visible and three in the infrared. Its orbit is 510 miles high. The path scanned is about

1,700 miles wide on the earth's surface. With this orbit and path width, all of the earth's surface is scanned in about twelve hours.

The geosynchronous satellites are much farther out in space. They are placed in an orbit 22,300 miles high, where their speed circling the earth exactly matches the earth's rotation speed ("geo" means earth and "synchronous" means matched in time). From this fixed position high above the earth, these satellites can view about one-fourth of the earth's surface. It is always the same one-fourth, since the satellite always stays in the same place. The time needed to scan the earth within their view depends only on the speed of the scanner and not the speed of the satellite, so the geosynchronous satellites give the fastest weather information.

The names of weather satellites that have been placed in geosynchronous orbit are the ATS (Applications Technology Satellites), the SMS (Synchronous Meteorological Satellites), and the GOES (Geostationary Operational Environmental Satellites). The SMS and GOES satellites normally give a new picture once every half hour. If meteorologists want pictures more quickly, the imaging system can be commanded by radio control to scan a smaller area. New pictures can then be received about once every three minutes.

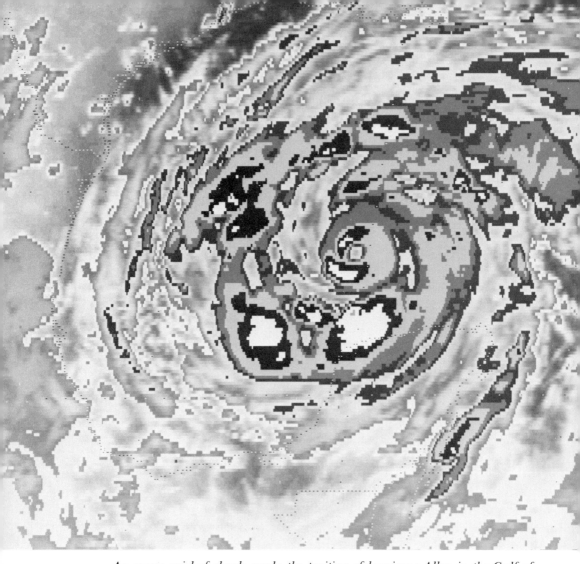

An angry swirl of clouds marks the position of hurricane Allen in the Gulf of Mexico in 1980, seen here in the infrared by the GOES weather satellite.

Meteorologists need many different types of information in their work. Pictures of cloud patterns are valuable for spotting storms, but clouds are not the cause of weather. They are only a sign of the powerful weather forces at work.

Other information needed is air temperature, pressure, humidity (the amount of water vapor in the air), wind speed and direction, heights and temperatures of the clouds, ground temperature, and the amount of energy from sunlight that is being absorbed by the earth.

Weather satellites use multi-spectral power to detect forces at work in the atmosphere above the earth in much the same way Landsat uses it to detect forces at work on the ground. Using infrared instruments sensitive to different wavelengths, weather satellites are able to measure many of the pieces of information meteorologists need (but not all: Air pressure, for example, can be guessed, but cannot be measured directly by satellite).

Besides providing weather and environmental information, these satellites do many other important jobs. They also act as communication satellites, receiving and rebroadcasting weather information from many ground weather stations that can't be reached directly. NOAA-8 also has a receiver to locate emergency radio signals from airplanes that have crashed. Weather satellites certainly rate as the most helpful of all our infrared eyes in space.

Spy Satellites

Military spy satellites have the most advanced infrared eyes in orbit. A satellite in space has a perfect view of earth. Traveling hundreds of thousands of miles a day, it can look into and photograph every country in the world. Airfields and airplanes, missile launch pads, ships, tanks, and trucks can be seen clearly in satellite photos.

The two main kinds of infrared spy satellites are early warning and reconnaissance. Early warning satellites search large areas of the earth looking for the bright flash that can mean an enemy missile has been launched. Rather than scan back and forth with a few infrared detectors, the way Landsat and weather satellites do, these satellites use large arrays of thousands of tiny detectors.

Arrays of detectors are like the human eye with its millions of sensors. Arrays can be scanned electronically at lightning speed instead of the slow back and forth of mechanical scanning. Like the human eye, arrays have both sharp vision and high speed. No missile launch can slip by while the scanner is looking the other way.

Reconnaissance satellites are purely for spying. Their orbits are lower than early warning satellites, so they can photograph every detail of secret military bases and other places of interest. Some reconnaissance satellites take pictures on film and then later drop the roll of film in a small can down to earth. As the can floats down by parachute, a military plane towing a net behind catches the film before it reaches the ground.

Other satellites record their pictures on a tape recorder

and later transmit them down to receiving stations as a television signal. How much reconnaissance satellites are able to see is a closely guarded secret. Some stories have said the satellite pictures are so clear and sharp it is possible to recognize people and even read automobile license plate numbers in them.

Infrared satellites are becoming the main eyes of modern defense. The countermeasures to these satellites (there are always countermeasures) are anti-satellite missiles and lasers. If a war were to break out, the first move by both sides would be to blind the "eyes" of the other.

DOWN TO EARTH

In the next chapter, we will drop down from space for a closer look at earth and see how infrared can save lives, save energy, and spot possible disasters in our homes and places of work before they happen.

EIGHT

Saving Lives and Energy with Infrared

IN THE growing darkness, a man and his son cling to the bottom of an overturned sailboat. Waves crash down on them, almost washing them into the sea. Their hands and arms ache from gripping the slippery hull and they are shaking with cold. Without help, there is no hope of their lasting through the night. And the man knows that no one will be able to find them in the darkness.

Then, over the howl of the wind, they hear the throb of a helicopter's rotor blades. A blinding searchlight blinks on, holding them in its beam as a Coast Guard crewman is lowered on a line. With practiced speed, the crewman helps them into a wire mesh rescue "basket." In a matter of minutes, they are hoisted to safety.

A powerful infrared "eye" inside the ball on the nose of this helicopter will help the Coast Guard see in the dark for rescue operations, law enforcement, and navigation.

"How did you ever find us in the dark?" the man shouts to one of the crewmen.

"With the FLIR," the crewman shouts back, pointing to a small television monitor in the cockpit. On the screen is a black-and-white television picture of the sea and coastline below them. Looking out the window, the eye can see nothing in the darkness.

Rescues like this will soon be commonplace. New FLIR (Forward Looking Infrared) systems are being built for Coast Guard helicopters to give them a powerful eye to see in the dark. The heart of this FLIR is an infrared imaging system that "sees" in the 8 to 14 micrometer wavelength region (the best region for looking at people and ground objects).

The Coast Guard FLIR is a ball-shaped turret that is

mounted to the nose of the helicopter. The FLIR operator inside the helicopter looks at a television screen and uses a small "joystick" to control the direction the turret is pointing. He can turn the turret to look at just one thing if he wishes or he can make the turret swivel from side to side and up and down to search over a wide area of ocean.

Besides search-and-rescue operations, the FLIRs will help in many of the other jobs the Coast Guard must handle. Drug smugglers trying to sneak boats into the country at night will discover that darkness no longer gives them cover to hide.

Ships that pump oil from their bilges into the sea will now be caught quickly and forced to pay high fines. Oil floats on top of water and, in the infrared, an oil slick appears as a dark patch on the ocean's surface. Nighttime navigation for the Coast Guard helicopters will also be safer with this new "eye."

HEAT MEANS TROUBLE

When you are sick, one of the first things a doctor wants to know is your temperature. A high temperature is an important sign that your body may be fighting a disease or an infection. Discovering an illness early can often prevent it from becoming serious later on.

High temperature can also be a sign of trouble with machines of all kinds. Engines, machinery, steam power

Dangerous problems that are invisible to the eye can often be spotted by infrared. High voltage electrical insulators appear normal in this visible photo.

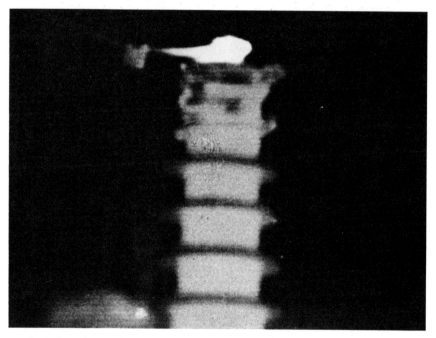

In the infrared, the wire on top of the insulator glows from overheating caused by a poor connection.

plants, and electrical motors and wiring often become hotter than normal when something is wrong. Spotting this over-heating early can prevent dangerous failures before they occur and save time, money, and sometimes even lives.

Infrared imaging systems that "see" in the 8 to 14 mi-crometer wavelength region are used for troubleshooting in many industries. From the infrared rays sent out by hot machinery, pictures of the heat patterns as well as tempera-ture measurements can be made quickly and safely from a long distance away or even from a helicopter or airplane.

Being able to measure temperature from a distance can be important when the "patient" is high voltage electrical wires, dangerous chemical or industrial processes, or ma-chinery spinning at high speed.

The infrared imaging systems made for inspecting in-dustrial plants are usually portable, battery-powered instru-ments that one person can carry. One looks like a small television camera. The operator points the "camera" at the machine he wants to check and looks at the infrared scene on a tiny television monitor. He sometimes records the pic-tures he sees on a video tape recorder to make a permanent record so that the pictures can be studied later.

SAVING ENERGY WITH INFRARED

In the winter, everything inside a warm, heated house glows in the infrared. If any heat is escaping around doors

Infrared shows heat loss patterns on the Massachusetts State House. The gold dome looks dark because it reflects the cold sky, while heat pours from the building face and the small windows below the dome.

or windows or through poor insulation in the walls or ceiling, those areas will be a little cooler and will look darker than the surrounding areas to an infrared imaging system.

From the outside, a well-insulated home or building will appear dark in the infrared. Bright areas are a sign of heat escaping from the inside. In hot summer weather, when buildings are air-conditioned, the temperature patterns will be the exact opposite.

A quick infrared inspection of a building or home can spot energy loss areas that would be difficult or impossible to find using any other method. Stopping energy loss can mean big savings in yearly heating or air-conditioning bills.

NINE

The World's Most Popular Guided Missile

How DOES an infrared-guided missile know which direction to fly? It knows because it can "see" infrared rays from the target aircraft's hot engine exhaust. The missile turns its fins to guide its flight path to the target. Being able to see and to guide makes the missile the most deadly weapon in modern warfare.

A rocket or a bullet simply goes in the direction it was pointed at the instant it was fired, but an infrared-guided missile is alive with an eye and a mind of its own. If the target tries to escape by turning or diving, a missile can see what is happening and follow the plane wherever it goes.

Infrared-guided missiles are especially important weapons to the military because they are completely "passive."

They do not need to send out a beam of energy that can warn the enemy the way "active," radar-guided missiles must. This makes infrared missiles difficult to detect and difficult to confuse with countermeasures.

THE BEGINNING OF AIRBORNE MISSILE WARFARE

Air warfare changed forever in 1958. In that year, a battle was being fought between Communist forces from the mainland of China and the Nationalist Chinese on the island of Taiwan. The Chinese Communist air force controlled the skies over the waters of the Formosa Strait between Taiwan and the mainland with large numbers of Russian-made MiG-17 fighters. The Nationalist Chinese, flying American-built F-86 Sabrejets were greatly outnumbered and the MiG-17 was thought by many to be a better aircraft.

In August, three American military officers and three civilian specialists from the Naval Ordnance Test Station, a navy airbase in the California desert, traveled to Taiwan. Together with a team of Marine and Air Force enlisted personnel, they put a new, secret weapon on the F-86s and taught the Chinese pilots how to use it. This new weapon was a missile called Sidewinder. It was named after a small desert rattlesnake that uses infrared to find and strike its prey.

In September, a flight of four F-86s escorting a supply

Sidewinder infrared-guided missiles arm the wing tips of this F-16XL fighter built for the Air Force.

convoy was attacked by about sixteen MiGs. During the battle, four (some stories say five) MiGs were shot down with Sidewinders. This battle marked the beginning of the end of Communist control of the Formosa Strait.

THE EYE OF A SIDEWINDER

The first Sidewinder wasn't very special-looking from the outside. It was just a white, metal tube, five inches in diameter and a little over nine feet long. It had four large, square fins on the tail and four small, triangle-shaped fins

93

near the nose. On the tip of the nose, there was a small, round window.

What was to make Sidewinder one of the most successful and most copied weapons in history lay inside the first twelve inches of the tube: in the guidance and control sections. The guidance section of a missile "sees" the target. The control section turns the wings to guide the missile to it.

The "eye" of a Sidewinder missile is a small telescope that collects infrared rays and focuses them onto a sensitive infrared detector. This telescope, or optical "head" as it is called, looks out through the window at the front of the missile. The missile's head is free to look to either side and up or down from the missile body.

The tail pipe(s) and exhaust gases at the back of a jet aircraft are very hot and send out large amounts of infrared. The infrared detector in a Sidewinder is made to be sensitive to those wavelengths where the rays from aircraft are strongest. To an infrared missile, a jet looks like a bright searchlight on a dark night.

When a strong infrared target like a jet is seen within the Sidewinder telescope's view, the optical head "locks on" and tracks the target, looking straight at it wherever it goes.

MISSILE GUIDANCE

Guidance is complicated when the target is a high-speed jet fighter. Even though the missile flies much faster than

A close up view of the deadly Sidewinder mounted on the wing launcher of a Navy F-14 Tomcat fighter.

An instant from destruction, a radio-controlled F-86 drone aircraft is intercepted by a Sidewinder missile.

the target, the rocket motor of the missile only burns for a few seconds. The missile must take the shortest route. If it flew straight toward the target, by the time it got there, the target would have moved ahead and the missile would have to turn and follow behind. This would be flying what is called a true pursuit course (pursuit means to chase).

Instead, the missile must head for the place where the target will be when the missile gets there. This is called a lead pursuit course. To lead the target this way, missiles use a kind of guidance called proportional navigation.

With proportional navigation, a missile flies so that the direction of the target (called the line of sight) doesn't change. Because the missile is flying toward where the target will be, rather than toward where it is at the moment, any

Impact! The F-86 erupts into a ball of flame.

maneuvers or turns by the target only shorten the distance the missile has to travel.

THE MOST POPULAR MISSILE

Since that first model, over 110,000 Sidewinders have been built in ten different models, including one called Chaparral that is launched from the ground. The infrared sensor in each new model has more sensitivity than the one before, so targets can be seen and shot at from greater distances.

Besides being used by the Navy, Marines, and Air Force of the United States, Sidewinder missiles are also used by the armed forces of twenty-seven other countries.

An early model of the Sidewinder is believed to have

been stolen and copied by Russia. This Russian model is called the AA-2 or Atoll missile. Atolls are used by the forces of at least thirty-three countries.

No country feels that its defenses are complete without large numbers of infrared missiles. In a world that is unable to live at peace with itself, infrared missiles are likely to be with us for a long time. Someday missiles may be replaced with a beam of energy that travels at the speed of light to destroy targets with pinpoint accuracy. This new super-weapon is the infrared laser.

TEN

The Infrared Laser: A Tool and a Weapon

IN A SHOWER of sparks, a sheet of steel is being sliced in two on a big machine. Where is the saw blade? There isn't one. Nothing is touching the metal, yet a cut is moving across the sheet like magic. A large, red sign on the wall of the room warns: "DANGER . . . Invisible Laser Radiation." Stand back, everyone! An infrared laser is at work!

THE POWER OF LIGHT

Have you ever taken a magnifying glass outside on a sunny day and focused the rays of sunlight down to a small spot on a piece of paper or wood? In less than a minute, smoke will begin to curl up and a burned spot will appear. Be careful, paper or wood may catch fire.

99

In a shower of sparks, an infrared laser drills holes in a steel plate.

Think about what has happened. Light from the sun has traveled 93 million miles across space and through earth's atmosphere and still has the power to burn. Multiply that power a few million times and you have an idea what a laser can do. A powerful laser beamed at a piece of wood will not just make the wood burn; it will make it explode.

The sun makes light from its heat, the same way a fire or the filament of a light bulb does. Chapter 4 showed the connection between the temperature of an object and the wavelengths of the rays the object sends out. Lasers make light (or infrared or ultraviolet rays) in a completely different way.

The word LASER comes from the first letters of "Light Amplification by Stimulated Emission of Radiation." That is quite a mouthful, but it just means to make light by pouring energy into a material (stimulating it) until it is full and has to dump all of its stored energy (the emission) as light rays.

Laser material changes the form of the heat or electricity or light energy put into it into pure light at just one wavelength. The wavelength of the laser's rays depends upon the kind of material used.

The first working laser was built in 1960 with a rod made of ruby that gave off red light. Since then, many materials have been found that can be used as lasers at wavelengths from the far-infrared to X-rays. Some of the most powerful lasers use a gas inside a tube as the laser material. The most powerful lasers of all right now are infrared.

High-energy lasers are still very large. The laser element itself is fairly small, but the power supply and the other equipment needed to operate it are large enough to fill a house.

LASER TOOLS

Being able to send energy from one place to another by a beam of light is what makes lasers so useful. A beam of light can be controlled with mirrors to move back and forth quickly over a big area and to focus to either a tiny spot or to spread out to a large one. Lasers are easily connected to computer-controlled machines to make robot machine tools for cutting, drilling, welding, and for hardening the surfaces of metals with high heat without warming up the metal inside.

Lasers are especially good for working on tiny parts. Holes as small as 0.002 inch across can be drilled. Because the work is done by a beam of light, there is no tool to wear out and have to be replaced. For materials that cannot be welded in air because of the oxygen, lasers can work in nitrogen or other gases that won't make the metal rust. Besides metals, lasers can also drill and cut ceramics, sapphires, and even diamonds.

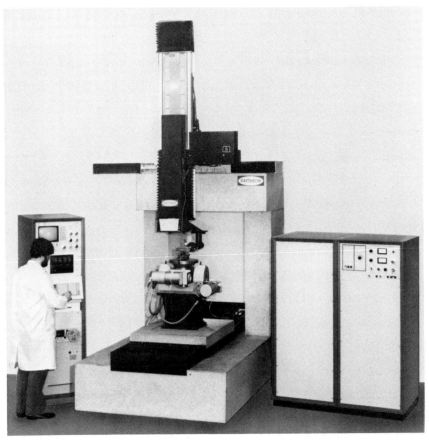

This powerful infrared laser machine tool can weld, cut, and drill extremely hard metals.

Laser Surgery

When a doctor operates on a patient to cut out cancers or tumors or stomach ulcers, stopping bleeding from the cuts can be a difficult problem. Now, doctors are beginning to use lasers instead of surgical knives for some kinds of operations.

Lasers are being used to cut out tumors in the brain and spinal cord that would normally be too dangerous to operate on. Lasers are also used on organs such as the stomach and spleen where bleeding is difficult to stop because of the many blood vessels. Lasers are likely to be used in any surgery where cuts must be made dangerously close to vital nerve centers or where bleeding is expected to be difficult to stop.

A laser doesn't cut by slicing as a knife does. A powerful laser vaporizes the body cells it strikes by burning them. The cells absorb the laser rays and instantly are heated to a high temperature that turns the liquid in the cells to steam. The laser "cut" seals itself, so bleeding is much less than with a knife cut.

Lasers can cut very precisely. Cells a few thousandths of an inch away from the cut are not harmed. Doctors often use a microscope to see and control the exact spot where the laser beam will be placed.

Lasers have another advantage over knives for surgery. Body cells are selective to the wavelengths of light they absorb. A doctor will choose a different laser for different types of operations. Three different lasers are most often used for surgery: argon lasers, carbon dioxide lasers, and

Nd:YAG (Neodymium:Yttrium-Aluminum Garnet) lasers.

Argon lasers give a visible, blue-green light at a wavelength of 0.5 micrometers. Hemoglobin in red blood cells absorbs green light. Agron lasers are used for operations on tiny blood vessels, on some kinds of birthmarks, and on the retina of the eye.

Carbon dioxide lasers are in the far-infrared at 10.6 micrometers. Water in body cells absorbs at this wavelength, making carbon dioxide lasers ideal for operations on brain tumors, muscle tissue, and some kinds of scars.

Nd:YAG lasers are in the near-infrared at a wavelength of 1.06 micrometers. Nd:YAG lasers penetrate deep into body tissue because both hemoglobin and water are fairly clear at 1.06 micrometers. This makes the Nd:YAG lasers useful for surgery of the stomach or the bladder where the laser beam must pass through liquid.

The rays from argon and Nd:YAG lasers can be sent through fiber optic bundles. Fiber optic bundles are made of thousands of tiny, flexible glass fibers that can carry light and near-infrared rays long distances and even around corners without greatly weakening the light's power. Doctors can use some of the fibers of a bundle to see through, others to shine a light to see by, and still others to carry the laser rays.

Operations can be done on some parts of the body without having to cut the patient open. For a stomach operation, a long, fiber optic bundle is passed down the patient's throat into the stomach. The doctor looks through the fiber optic. When he finds the area he wants to operate on, he presses a switch that causes a pulse of laser energy to be sent down the fiber optic.

Both visible and infrared lasers will be used for surgery more and more in the future as lasers become less expensive and as new, smaller lasers are designed that can be used in areas of the body that are difficult to reach. Lasers that can be tuned to different wavelengths will make use of the body's natural selective absorption of laser light.

LASER COMMUNICATION

Laser beams can be used like radio waves to send voice and television signals. One laser beam can carry thousands more channels than a radio wave can. Most laser communication systems use infrared lasers at a wavelength of 1.06 micrometers.

Lasers can be beamed through the air between two places that are within sight of each other. Laser messages can also be sent through fiber optic bundles under city streets and inside buildings, the same as telephone wires. Fiber optic bundles are lighter, more flexible, and one day will be cheaper than wire cables for communications.

As more and more communication is between computers rather than between people, there is a need for more communication channels and higher and higher speeds. Work is under way now to develop a laser fiber optic cable to be laid under the ocean to link America and Europe with more channels than present wire cables and communication satellites can carry.

LASER POINTERS FOR THE MILITARY

The narrow beam that lasers send out makes them useful to the military as range finders and as target designators. Soldiers use portable infrared lasers that look like short, fat rifles with a large telescope on top. These range finders and designators work in the near-infrared at 1.06 micrometers, so their rays are invisible to the eye.

Because their beams are very narrow, these lasers can shine a small spot of laser light on a single target such as an enemy tank several miles away. When used as a range finder, the laser sends out pulses of light and receives the reflection of the light back. By electronically measuring the time needed for the light to travel to the target and back, distance can be calculated very accurately. This distance can then be used to aim artillery guns.

When used as a target designator, a soldier points the laser at the target. The laser light reflected from the target can be "seen" by infrared sensors in a laser-guided artillery shell, missile, or bomb. These laser-guided weapons can be launched from many miles away and hit small targets with pinpoint accuracy.

LASER WEAPONS

Laser weapons of all kinds are going to be very much in the news for the rest of this century. High-energy lasers, or "directed-energy weapons" as they are called in the military, offer one of the best hopes of a defense against enemy ICBMs (Inter-Continental Ballistic Missiles) carrying atomic warheads.

High-energy, infrared laser weapons are being built and tested now at several places in the United States and in the Soviet Union. Laser weapons are also being tested in aircraft. In tests in California in May of 1983, an infrared laser carried in a large NKC-135 (a military Boeing 707) jet shot down five Sidewinder missiles as they streaked through the air.

In the future, more advanced and powerful lasers than these may be put into orbit in space. These laser battle sta-

Laser battle stations in space may one day be our main defense against enemy missiles.

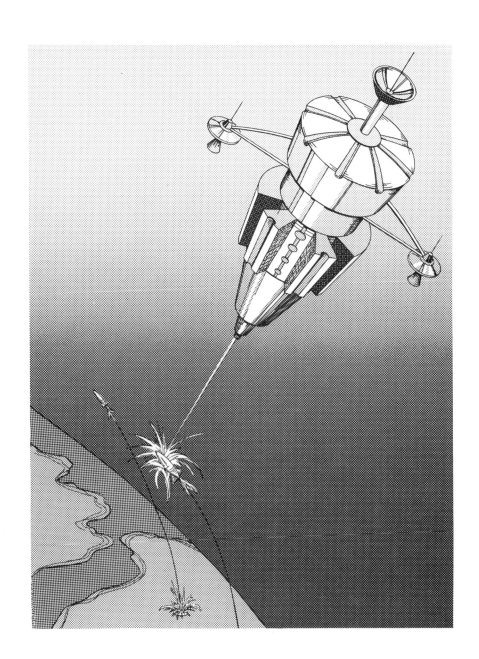

tions could become our main defense against missiles and against spy satellites.

The research and design for these lasers are pushing back the limits of what is possible. Though these lasers are being designed for the military, there will be advances in laser surgery for medicine, in power transmission by laser light instad of electric wires, in astronomy from space telescopes, in laser mining, in laser machining, and in many other fields because of this work.

A Bright Future with Lasers

What will the future be like? Of course, no one knows for certain, but new inventions and new machines to help us are being made ever faster and faster. Infrared lasers will become more useful and more used as their prices and their size comes down.

Someday we may have many laser appliances around the house carrying television and telephone signals, cutting up material for sewing, slicing up food for cooking, and doing dozens of other cutting and cleaning chores. How would you like to have a laser lawn mower to cut the grass?

Right now is one of the most exciting times of all to be alive. In the next chapter, let's take a fun trip into our future with infrared.

ELEVEN

Infrared in Your Future

WHAT ARE the weirdest, wildest machines you can imagine? Whatever they are, you can be sure that the future will have things even more fantastic. No one can tell what kind of machines we will be using in ten or twenty or fifty years. But if we follow the direction pointed by what is happening today, we can have fun guessing about tomorrow.

The biggest changes happening right now are in computers. New computers are being made and new uses for computers are being found every day. We have video games, home computers, pocket calculators, and wristwatch calculators that no one dreamed possible fifteen years ago. At that time computers were giant-sized and cost thousands of dollars. Computers that were not as good as the ones you can buy at a toy store today filled a room then, and a really large computer filled a whole building.

The main thing that has brought computers out of the laboratories and into our lives is their low price. If something can be made cheaply enough so that a large number of people can afford it, it will find a place in the home.

Today, infrared cameras and instruments are so expensive that only businesses and the military can afford them. But when their prices come down, and they will before long, you will find machines using infrared in every house, car, plane, and boat.

MACHINES THAT SEE AND THINK

One of the most exciting uses for infrared is putting infrared "eyes" into computers to make robots that can see and think. The infrared devices that will make that possible are large detector arrays: thousands or tens of thousands of tiny infrared detectors made on one "chip" of transistor material. Large detector arrays are being made now for the military for reconnaissance systems and spy satellites. When the cost of these arrays comes down, it will be possible to have infrared eyes everywhere.

Computers don't really think, not the way we do, but they can remember things and compare one thing to another and make programmed decisions. To compare pictures, either visible or infrared, a computer uses what is called "pattern recognition" to find out if the image seen with its detectors is the same as any of the pictures stored in its memory.

The image the computer sees doesn't have to match exactly one of the pictures in its memory for a computer to identify it. The computer looks for parts that look the same as those in its memory and gives the scene a grade for how much the two pictures are alike. It can be programmed to accept pictures that are close, but not exactly the same.

If you were given the job of spotting trucks going by on the street, your brain would also use pattern recognition. You know what a truck looks like. Even though trucks come in all sizes, shapes, and colors, you would have no trouble.

How do you do this? By comparing every part of the thing you see, from the overall shape to each of the small parts, with your memories of all the other trucks you have seen. You don't give the picture a number grade in your mind the way a computer would. Humans don't think in numbers like that, but the end result would be exactly the same.

No computer built is as good as your brain at pattern recognition. Being able to pick out very complicated shapes happens to be a special human gift. Most "seeing" jobs for computers must be kept fairly simple, but computers are getting more advanced all of the time.

The Robot with the Infrared Eyes

Take some infrared detectors for the eyes, add a computer for the brain, "robotics" programming for the computer, mechanical hands to grasp and pick up things, and legs or wheels to move around, and you can have a complete, useful robot. Imagine what kinds of things a robot that can see in the dark could do.

How would you like to have your own personal robot? You could call him or her (are robots usually boys or girls?) when you wanted chores done. You could play cards or a video game with your robot if you got bored, or take it out with you at night as a body guard. With infrared eyes, it could see in the dark as well as the daylight.

We usually think of robots as having one head and the same number of arms and legs as we do, but they don't have to. Robots can have as many arms and legs and eyes in as many different designs as needed to do a job.

If you were repairing a small machine or sewing with a needle and thread, think how handy it would be to have eyes in the tips of your fingers. Or to have a third arm, perhaps connected to the top of your head, so you could hold small parts in front of your eyes while you worked on them with your other two hands. Or to have separate brains in each of your hands so they could work on their own and leave the brain in your head free to think of other things.

114

Personal robots with infrared vision are not far in the future. This little robot you can buy today can sense light, speak to you, hear sounds, and be programmed to do simple jobs.

And Leave the Driving to Us

A computerized robot that can "see" images the way we do could drive a car on any street, probably more safely than a human could. Robots don't get tired or forget to pay attention. A special-purpose robot like this wouldn't be made human-shaped with arms and legs and a head. It would most likely be built into a box somewhere in the car.

The box would hold its computer brain. Its "eyes" and "ears" would be all around the car connected to the brain by wires. Just jump into your car, tell it where you want to go, and sit back and relax. And, with infrared eyes, your car wouldn't need headlights to drive at night.

Goodbye, Burglars

With a "seeing-eye robot" guarding your home, you would never have to worry about the wrong person getting inside. The robot's computer brain would be programmed to keep out anyone who didn't look like your family and friends.

With infrared vision, the robot couldn't be fooled by disguises. A mask or false nose or false mustache or any other disguise would have a different temperature pattern than a normal human face.

The same idea might be used by the police to find criminals. Robot scanners could be used in busy places like airports and bus stations to look at everyone that passed and to sound an alarm when they saw someone like the person they were looking for.

SUPERWEAPONS

The weapons of the future won't be bigger and bigger bombs. They will be smaller and smarter missiles that will know exactly what their targets look like. These missiles will hunt until they find the targets they were programmed for, and they could wait patiently for years until the right target comes along.

Anti-aircraft missiles will look for airplanes and be able to tell enemy planes from friendly ones. Anti-tank missiles will look for enemy tanks and anti-ship missiles for ships. Defenses will be more automatic than ever before possible. With infrared detectors for eyes, these missiles will work day and night and will be able to see through most kinds of camouflage.

Tomorrow's military will use laser weapons more powerful and more accurate than anything we have today. Lasers will be used on airplanes, ships, tanks, and aboard space satellites. If the problems of storing large amounts of energy in some kind of small "power pack" can be solved, laser rifles and pistols may be carried by soldiers in the field.

The accuracy of these lasers will completely change the

way wars are fought. Large numbers of soldiers will never be used together. Wars will be fought by small groups that can stay hidden as much as possible. With a laser weapon, if a target can be seen, it can be hit in an instant. There will be no misses and no second chances in future wars.

A RAY OF HOPE

What will our lives be like surrounded by "smart" machines that can see in the dark? From what has happened in the past with inventions like electricity, airplanes, and automobiles, we can guess that the future will be filled with new challenges, new dangers, and new freedoms.

The industrial machine age has freed us from most of the heavy, backbreaking factory work. The personal machine age that is coming will free our homes and the other parts of our lives.

Don't worry about machines taking over the world. New machines always make more jobs than they take away, because, with them, it becomes possible to do things we would never have dreamed of before. Having machines to do the boring work will leave us free to do the things humans are best at: the things that machines can never do.

When an idea pops into your head, when you string together words to make a story or musical notes to make a song, when you feel a happy or a sad feeling, when you

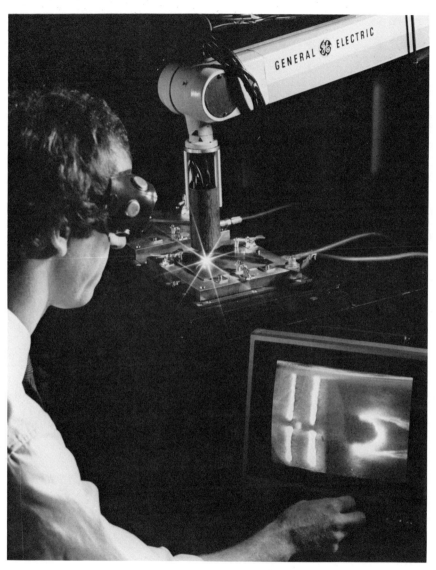

This industrial robot uses the power of sight and a computer brain to guide a welding arm along the correct path.

dream by day or by night, you are performing a kind of magic in your mind that can't happen any place else.

The biggest and richest universe of all is the one inside your own head. All great art and ideas and discoveries and inventions start right there, just behind your eyes. And just in front of your eyes, the whole visible and invisible world begins, waiting to be explored. With a little help from the machines we build, the world of the infrared will no longer be invisible.

Index

Page numbers in italics indicate illustrations

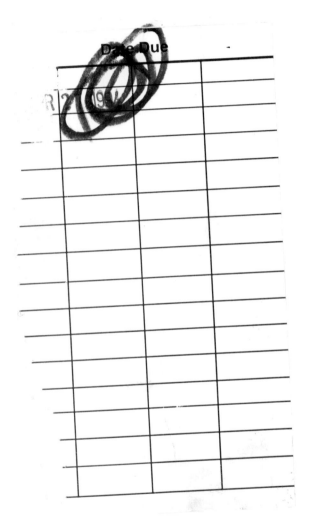